AF484586

DarkHeartandMind

For the Emotionally Complex

Mitchell One

BookLeaf Publishing

India | USA | UK

Copyright © Mitchell One
All Rights Reserved.

This book has been self-published with all reasonable efforts taken to make the material error-free by the author. No part of this book shall be used, reproduced in any manner whatsoever without written permission from the author, except in the case of brief quotations embodied in critical articles and reviews.

The Author of this book is solely responsible and liable for its content including but not limited to the views, representations, descriptions, statements, information, opinions, and references ["Content"]. The Content of this book shall not constitute or be construed or deemed to reflect the opinion or expression of the Publisher or Editor. Neither the Publisher nor Editor endorse or approve the Content of this book or guarantee the reliability, accuracy, or completeness of the Content published herein and do not make any representations or warranties of any kind, express or implied, including but not limited to the implied warranties of merchantability, fitness for a particular purpose.

The Publisher and Editor shall not be liable whatsoever...

Made with ❤ on the BookLeaf Publishing Platform
www.bookleafpub.in
www.bookleafpub.com

To the Divine Universe. To my family and friends who have all my love. To the moments that couldn't break me, and especially to the moments that made me.

Acknowledgement

I want to acknowledge that I found this opportunity because Bookleaf posted this challenge on their social media and I saw it and actually did it! So, shout out to the positive use of social media!

Preface

Poetry has had a profound effect on me since I was a kid, yet calling myself a poet isn't something I feel comfortable doing just yet. I never knew who all the cool poets were, nor knew of the ones I was supposed to know. I don't even think I could say I have a favorite poet. I just loved the concept of rhyming words, which would eventually inspire making Hip-Hop music. On a break right now, but writing raps was originally seen as just writing poems alongside beats. Free verse was such an interesting area of poetry when I discovered it as an early teen. "Poems are supposed to rhyme" is what I initially thought to myself in grade school. Very glad I dropped that obsolete thought pattern.

My point is that while I know my way around a stanza or two, it is intimidating to be writing poetry, publish a book of poems, and therefore be considered a poet. I have a background in acting and have fully immersed myself in Shakespeare multiple times now. Actually writing something myself has been a challenge and an amazing blessing.

Now to the work itself. DarkHeartandMind is a series of poems, mostly new works with some old pieces thrown in as well, detailing my unadulterated thoughts and emotions. Said thoughts and emotions are weaved into these poems with as much clarity, honesty, and authenticity that I can poetically provide. There wasn't a clear story to tell per se, as much as there was a running theme throughout; glimpsed in the direct nature of the title. I cannot speak for anyone else truthfully, but the sheer intensity of existence has me losing my mind. Insane part being that I'm losing my mind as I become increasingly aware of how sane I am in comparison to members of my own species. Art is a wonderful method to express one's abstract internal turmoil, where logic just simply doesn't suffice.

"Full of internal turmoil" could be the epitaph on my tombstone. I don't imagine I'm alone in that, but herein the work is all mine. Topics within this book are broad and range from spirituality/religion, race, class, sex, sexuality and romance to name a few. You'll find far more than a simple analysis of all the isms that permeate and run a muck within our society though. There is a carnal and crude nature suffused amongst the civil base. I wanted to "keep it real", as much as I could anyway, as I try to still respect and honor the natures of poetry that I love. It also isn't all tortuous, emo, melodrama either. There are spots of genuine love and happiness inside too.

All that said, I only really have one more thing to say. In the words of queen Erykah Badu "I'm an artist and I'm sensitive about my shit" but I'm also no coward. I respect that while these works solely belong to me, I am sharing them with you, the reader, in full confidence. My sincerest hope is that it touches you, resonates, and provides an eccentric beauty that helps you step into your own power and affect positive change in yourself and surroundings.

Begrudged Beginning

Hard start
Hard to start
In the first place
In the beginning
Formless and empty
Ex nihilo
Alive and well
Yet maybe
Empty still
Primordial I
Wonders why
Live says life
Air watching you die
Thankful to draw breath
Am I?
Ungrateful
Uncouth
Uncomfortable us all
It seems now
Slavery built the Pyramids
Crossed the Atlantic
Got lost
In this amazing black woman's railroad

Chit chatting about capital the whole time
Slavery switched to taxes
The back scratches
Were not taken in kind
Capitalism's the new errand boy
Capitalizing on a far too human trend
Devaluing the priceless human life
Renegotiating my worth
Over and over and over and over and over
Again
Have you ever thought of
Returning the greatest gift ever given?
Felt the shame
Run down your spine at the very thought?
Impossibly complex world we live in
Hope you aren't as hard on yourself as I
My rage at it all could burn hell
Damn whatever allowed all this mess
Thankful to know life is sacred
I'm gonna keep living I guess

Heart Beside Heart

Her body naked in my arms for
Fingers to caress
Legs wrapped around my naked
Self to sleep away unrest
Laid down atop fresh linen
Her hand upon my chest
Breast perked against breast
Her warmth holds me the best
My soul heated to fire now
Skin prickling at the seams
Faster I'd rather melt down
Than to wake this beautiful
Queen
Faster I'd rather melt down
Than to wake from this beauteous
Dream
Lips close enough to touch
No illusion this is
Real
I thank the heavens a thousand times
I'll never forget the way this angel
Feels

With Great Power

Who I am
Has never mattered more than
Who I want to be
Iniquity runs rampant
Rampaging through
My world
My country
My state
My city
Morale not very high
It's not that serious
Some may say
I would say
Docility
Is a trick of the oppressor
Their favored state of being
In those they seek to oppress
What I don't want
Is to be docile
While simultaneously stressed
The best I can be
Is what I seek
When evil rears its ugly head

Cut off the head
That it may grovel instead
I owe this to myself
To my family, my friends
Acquaintances, strangers
They owe it back to me as well
Shared responsibility
From the ability within me
Out to the ability within you
What world do we choose?
Thanks Uncle Ben

Gods to Humans

Goddess bless me
I've forgotten my face
What dimension is this
Plain this plane
Sanity is slipping
I descend
The golden chain?
No
A lotus petal erupts
Out of my navel?
No
A jeweled spear
I stir the landless ocean
I can't remember
Ambrosia and nectar
No
I eat of the fruit
Knowledge
Denied the fruit of life
Banished from paradise
No!
I am divine!
I am the universe!

I...feel
Alive but
Weak
Cold
Slowly dying
Very
Very
Slowly
Goddess our connection
Faint
Where are you?
Why can't I hear you?
I am lost
I am scared
I'm...
Late to work again
Shit
I can't lose this job man
I'm already behind on rent
The baby needs food
My car needs gas
Aight let's go
Wait wasn't I doing something?
Ugh never mind it doesn't
Matter

Choice is Yours

Life is hard, yet also soft
Metaphor or literal
Take it serious maybe scoff
Kill or be killed or trivial
Serial or cereal
Food for thought absent mind
Stolen goods lucky find
Nature versus nurture
Are we animal
Perhaps more civilized
Complexity surmised
Simplicity pretends a lot
Forward back
Directionless
Goddess
God
Man
Will you
Stand
Fall
Will

Let White Hate Go

Made you look
Nah just playin
But also sayin
I ain't playin
Massa's game
For I refuse
To be a slave
No longer confused
I can't move the same
Segregation and hatred
Was apart of massa's plan
So together we would never stand
United
I choose to elevate
Remove the shackles
Off my brain
Tackle conflicting emotions
Heal all my pain
I will not ignore history
Wrongs
Must
Be made
Right

Fight always the oppression
Laden with humanity's
Past mistakes
Eurocentricity is last century's error
Fairer skin bias
A slowly dying fate
Wake up to truth
Be made whole
Divided is not the goal so
Let go of the hate
Waste of energy
The masters wanted you drained
To bring disaster even from the grave
Brave the world with love instead
Let us bring the dead masters
To their eternal shame

Hearth of Heart

North
West
East
South
Travel is lovely
Yet just as well a house
Unravel this mystery
A house furnished yet empty
Gently one wanders about
Coarse is the course of course
Something is missing
You require fire
A heart set ablaze in love
We're not burning the house down
Don't be silly
Be willing
To add your warmth
Here is where you rest your heart
Let down your sorrows and worry
Forget the need to rush
Hush now child
Have no fear
You left outside out there

It's only friends and family here
Life is not always fair
Can't say this will be a perfect place
Can you settle for a wonderful space?
Smile from ear to ear?
Do you like to play games?
Perhaps a nice meal?
A beer?
The house was never empty
You were just cold
Bold of you to feel so alone
It doesn't take much
To make a house a home
The hearth is very hot now
Here there's no need to detach
A beautiful flame engulfs us all
We never struck a single match

Loving Lewd

Lascivious lust
Leave me be
Or pass me
A clutch of
Mardi gras beads for
Beautiful bare breasts
A pleasure to see
Fat bottomed girls
Also make me come alive
Just a man dreaming
He may cum inside
Tight walls dripping arousal
Passionately my tongue teases
Clitoral stimulation
I do believe it pleases
With pornographic intent
Hell bent on climax for
All the time spent
Why feel shame
Of any kind?
Am I whore for
Giving in to sexual desire?

Or is it wearing women's thighs
As earmuffs?
Drowned by womanhood
Is my choice your honor
I plead guilty
But she and
All women like her
Are innocent
Fine selling her vagina for
Male gaze and attention
Madness when she decides
Only for her fans
Free her nipples
Why censor beauty
Natural or otherwise?
You were fine suckling
On and around her areolas
But nursing her child
An abomination?
When nations can only be birthed
By the very milk of a woman's teat?
Listen you freaks
A woman's body can go from
Short to tall
Skinny, fit or thick

Busty to smaller cupped
Little to big butts
And everything in between
My imagination runs rampant
Creating all the sexual scenes
All the while remembering
A woman owes me nothing
Outside my own dreams

May I Die by the Sword Please?

The Pen is
Mightier than the sword
So they say
Yet people
Live and die by it
Everyday
"Niggas get shot everyday b"
As Rico once said
Memorialize their names
Murals on the wall
Hopeful litigation
That sometimes help
Other times fall short
I'm a tough enough nigga it turns out
Guess I'll be alright
Yet is that what I'm supposed to be?
Wielding the mightiest pen
Was a true goal of mine
Once upon a time
These days I aim for the biggest stick

Not talking about my dick either
You see
Power is what rules our world
Shame in fact
Begrudgingly keeps the world intact
Destroying little by little all the while
I'm not sure my pen is
Equipped to handle the pressure
Perhaps I simply feel better with
Weapon in hand to meet my demands
Simple straightforward interaction
Death by my sword or
Death under yours
Survivor keeps the spoils to
Spoil those they see fit
My sword would spoil our world
That we may never live as
Facsimiles of broken system
After broken system
Godkings to
Emperors to
Nation Kings to
Prime Ministers to
Presidents
The precedent embarrassing

Who in right mind
With power
Glowers over another human being and
Sees a resource
Rather than
A source of ascension for the
Human species?
Evil won't respect my pen and
I can't live like this much longer
This isn't properly living at all
So I will stand tall
Courageous through my immense fear
Slam myself against the wall of iniquity
Despite these angry tears
And die on my shield
Please

4 Brothers

Live for my brothers
Fight for my brothers
Care for my brothers
Die for my brothers
Blood in with three brothers
Shed blood for
My different mother brothers
Point is
Love for my brothers
Wisdom from my eldest
Discipline from my elder
Growth because of the youngest
Eccentricity from me
Madness permeates my mind
My brothers ground me
Madness awkwardly channeled
Transmuting insanity into
Curiosity flowing
Towards artistic endeavor
From boys
Spanked for gaming after bedtime
To men
Navigating disparate paths into adulthood

From alt black angsty teen
To an alt black uncle
Troubled by what the future may bring
Dream chasing chasms of distance
Lessened by the covenant of Thanksgiving
Thankful no matter how far and wide
Brothers, my brothers
Still by my side
Ready to ride
My chosen extended family true
My gifted brothers few
Nameless they shall remain but
To Shadow, T, and P-Hustle
I thank
I love
I live and die for
You
Love
My dear brothers
Eternal

I Would've Liked a Sister

No sisters growing up
Hard to miss something
You never had
Doting older sister
Doting on baby sister
Would I have been able to
Handle the stark contrast
Between my parents rearing
Haitian sons versus
Haitian daughters?
Would my older sister hate me?
Freedoms given to me younger
Though she was responsible for me
Years prior as a baby boy
Mom and Dad definitely
Nitpick at my attire far less as well
My puppy love girlfriends
Considered cute
Baby sis tried the same
Dad was ready to shoot
Older or younger
Sis isn't getting the same liberties
Freed ourselves from French masters

Only to limit our own women
Treated like queens and princesses
Of course
The crown still a cage
Behave or be sent to Haiti
Any Haitian parent to
Any misbehaving Haitian child
Manouchka
Wanted to hang with her friends
After school
Just for a little bit
She forgot to tell
Mom and Dad
They made me get the belt
And after not sparing her the rod
We sat in the living room
Praying over her all night
Grandma with us
Aunty still on the phone from
Mom's earlier gossiping
Dad hasn't stopped glaring since we started
She hasn't stopped crying
I sneak into her room to give her a hug
Parents are tough on me too but
Not like this

No sisters growing up
Hope I saved her a headache at least

Ayiti my Dear

L'Union Fait La Force
Of course
I know the motto
By heart
Not as well it's land
My start is as
An American
Funny
To be made
To pledge allegiance
To your mother country's
Greatest agitator
Playing a friend
While subtly
Having his way with her
Mocks in media's mood
Rude
And still this is my home
Sheltered away
As my parents home
Still lay under siege
Ayiti toujou kanpe
Kreyòl shouts

Inside my head
There is a divide
Dan ké m
Liberty and justice for all
I don't know the Haitian national anthem
By heart but
Libète pou Ayiti

WitchBoy

Charged by
The Goddess
Queen of all witches
Aligned along
The path of
The Horned One
Guardian of all things wild and free
Shouting so loud
Into the void
The Great Old Ones
May hear my cries
As I
Reach towards she
The Goddess
Who I affirm as
Nana Buluku
Mother Goddess
Who birthed
Mawu-Lisa
Twin sun and moon
Grandmother of
The Orisha
Who traveled the lands

And became
The Lwa
Of Ayiti
Bringing Vodou
Into my bloodline
Ogou Feray
Guardian Lwa by my side
Magick
Suffusing my being
Dancing with
Dragons
Unwinding with
Unicorns
Frolicking with
Fae
Calling on the elements
To empower my way
Earth
Air
Fire
Water
Spirit
The tie that binds
This human matrix
Pentacle

Branded to my back
That I may never forget
Just missing the cat
Hoping perhaps
Bastet
Blesses me with
A friendly familiar
Harnessing the
Divine destruction of
Shiva
Next on my list
Black boy joy throughout
This eclectic mix
Scoff, doubt, call me insane
I'd rather bathe naked
In moonlight
Than straddle
The mundane

Read it and Weep

When did your existential crisis begin?
Asked a brave therapist to a sad adult me
Sitting solemnly in front of her
I said maybe about 4 years old maybe five
To which she obviously replied
Why?
To which I said
That's around the age I learned to read
Although it could be sooner
Since my father was ensuring
We knew the Holy Bible
Before we knew how
We knew the Holy Bible
Genesis alone got me thinking
God got over on humanity and
Now we all suffer for one mistake?
And then we get to traditional history
Where you get to read about how many times
Humanity refuses to be better than itself
Thank the Goddess history also
Records revolutions otherwise
I would have jumped
Off a bridge a long time ago

I guess even the Bible gave us Yeshua
A tale of empathy and compassion
Far removed from the flood
To punish the corrupt or
The wrath upon Sodom and Gomorrah
Point is doc
I say to a now concerned therapist
Literacy is as important as freedom
Damned
If it doesn't have a double edge though
You aren't actually going to jump off a bridge
Right?
Says the mental health professional
To her patient
I don't really know sometimes
I silently think
Just tired of crying inside
I say aloud
Ok then let's pick this up in 2 weeks
Says the now relieved therapist
And the session ends

Silent Rain Drops

Rain drops
Falling on my head
No umbrella
Drip drip drip
The intrusive thought just now
Was a very inappropriate
Chappelle Show quote
Lost in thought
Day to day
Sunup to sun down
Why would you hit that person for
No reason?
No don't drive into that river
You cannot just kiss that woman
She does not know you
Why are you thinking about
Kissing that guy?
If your gay be gay
But pretending for
Mental discourse is tiring
You cannot fight ten men
At once Bruce Leeroy
It literally is trash

You would throw up
Before it even touches your lip
Don't kill anyone
Don't kill yourself
Murder is immoral and illegal
Remember?
Shhhhh
Please
Just be quiet
It's too nice a sunny day
To wallow in rain

#Giveafuck

I used to
Want to be
Too cool for school
Liked by the hottest girls
Looked up to by lower grades
Envied and/or feared by competition
At least in the smallest
Piece of my consciousness
High key ashamed for the want at all
Shitty behavior
I never actually
Acted that way tho
Thank the Goddess
What a bitch Id be
Or be pretending to be
When did not caring
Become some stoic sign of coolness
I mean
Maybe for chasing love interests
Who take your loving interest
For granted
They know they don't have to

Work for you
Chase is gone
As well as counter interest
Damn that mentality
Ungrateful bastards
Us all
Care for
Christ's sake
Excitement at
The most minuscule
Light a got damn fire
In your chest
Let passion fill you to the brim
Acting cool is for fools
Actually being cool
In authenticity
Is how we must live
In the flesh

Rage Tipped Spear

Keep it all inside
Right in your body
Bide your time
Let emotion build
If you waste it all
On every stimuli
Crossing your path
What will you have
When the worst comes
Peace is a lie
Passion your guide
Strength flows through you
Power builds in time
Scary part that power
Pursuit of it
A corrupting influence
Since the dawn of humankind
Focusing that power
In the right direction
The only honest option
All the struggle
All the pain
All the time spent

Bringing you to now
When the time comes
You cannot fail
Do not waste
Precious energy
On the infantile and incompetent
But on your enemies
Seen or unseen
An unstoppable combatant
Battle worthy virtuoso
A panther
Always at the ready
To pounce
Do not
Waste the rage
Strike true where it matters
Usher us into
A new age

Paralysis

Is it my shame
To be alive?
Mostly safe
Less so
In the confines
Of my own mind
I should be Luigi
But am I ready?
What life does one live
As a pariah?
I guess otherwise a life
Filled with indecision
Filled with regret
Filled with hesitation
Filled with lack of action
Inertia
Einsteinian explanation
Unnecessary
Blocking myself
From moving
The movement forward
I ain't Huey P Newton
I ain't Malcolm X

Certainly not Martin Luther King Jr
Could I have even
Been as brave as Rosa Parks?
Fred Hampton
Assassinated at twenty one
Spent his life doing the right thing
Killed cause wrong won that day
I'm scared
Everyday I wake
Descended from people
Following Toussaint L'Ouverture
In battle against Napoleon Bonaparte
But I barely follow my own heart
Move!
Move!!!
Mooooove!!!!!
The world won't wait for you

Blackheart

I just got this
Black spot
Where
My heart
Used to be
Blessed truly
Yet somethings off
Brother Baldwin
Would say
Im experiencing a
Constant state of rage
Consciously aware of the
World around me
Complexity simplified
Yet the current state of
My country
States that
Comprehension is not
The problem
Kinda cold blooded now
Can't let these thieves
Believe they've taken my joy
But I do find myself

Touching my chest
Just to feel a beat
Ba dum ba dum
Beats the drum
The metaphor
Becoming the percussion
My ancestors played
Invigorating the spirit
That the flesh may follow
How low
We've fallen
Undefeated still
Yet always watching
Per chance of demise
I'm not as strong as you
Sister Angelou
Even knowing
I must still rise
Rise to the occasion then
Maya breathes into me
This hurting black man
That heart's as good as any
She says
So here now I stand
Black

Bold
Beautiful
Free

HateEater

Transmutation
Change something
Into another form
Lead to gold
Human life to homunculi
How about
Hate to love
Or at least fuel
As your enemies
Brandish the tool
To end your existence
I
Mitchell
Joseph
One
Am the
Hate Eater
Feed me
You despicable fools
Come with weapon
Every kind
Slander
Every shape

Method after method
Will not take
I seal your fates
Gnash gunpowder
Against my gums
Fire breathing
Truth spitter
As your slurs fall short
As your glares graze against my shadow
As your hate fails against my unyielding soul
Bitter the taste of the thought
You will never
Ever
Ever
Ever
Win
You so full of sin within
Doesn't take the Bible
To read you
Yet the masses pretend
But I
Am still here
Bathed in darkness
As I continue righteously toward the light
Spiritual warrior

Beaten not broken
Until this world is made right

Everlasting

When the life goes out of my eyes
Will you remember me?
Will you hold me in high esteem?
Hold me as the last vestiges of life
Leave me an empty vessel
Who once upon time
Walked this blessed Earth?
I for one hope not
For I would hope
You have something more precious
Validation?
Legacy?
What are these concepts
If not a little human's fear
At the expanse of existence and
Their place in it all
Creation
Falling
Rising
Destruction
We are more than a cyclical pattern
The universe expresses so much
Here we are amongst the dust

Just getting by?
If I die before I wake
Whether in my sleep or
Misfortunate mistake
Promise you will set me aside
Live in
Love
Strength
Wisdom
Light the hearth of heart inside
Courageous when facing fear
Fighting till your last breath for
Everything you hold dear
We are everything not nothing
We are family not strangers
We are the light in the dark
We are the dark in the light
We are animals
We are civilized
We are base
We are divine
And we are certainly not finished
Let us joins hands
Lift every voice and sing

Let us reach our fullest potential
Virtuosity
Everlasting

www.ingramcontent.com/pod-product-compliance
Lightning Source LLC
Chambersburg PA
CBHW061719130726

47996CB00006B/2403